Kindle Paperwhite User Guide:

An Easy-and-Quick-to-Use

Kindle Paperwhite E-reader Guide

TABLE OF CONTENTS

INTRODUCTION

In this technology era, e-readers have since 2007 changed the reading experience. Currently, the Kindle Paperwhite provides the best option when it comes to e-readers. In support of its quality, Amazon states that this Kindle Paperwhite directs light towards the display in order to ensure your comfort when reading your library of books. The e-reader allows you to download and have access a selection of titles while at your comfort zone.

Amazon, the sole producer of this device, do not provide printed manuals to help the users maximize on its quality. Fortunately, to enjoy the above-mentioned advantages among the many others, this book provides the important guides that will enable you to enhance your reading experience. That is, the book explains the preliminary activities to help you get started. This involves setting up the Kindle Paperwhite, as well as detailed explanations of all the important features of the Kindle Paperwhite e-reader.

Special instructions to allow you to understand easily the content of the Kindle document is one important determinant to attract you into purchasing the e-reader. Guidelines on how to select quality e-reader and where to find them are as well provided in this special book. For example, the ability to customize the text display makes it qualify as the best e-reader at an affordable price in this era.

To make your reading on the go, it is important to go through this guidebook keenly. Failure to which you would miss to experience the potential of this Amazon device in whatever environment you are in. Understand the detailed information about the Kindle Paperwhite in order to modernize yourself with the updated version of the e-reader for a promising scholarly future.

In case you need to acquire an e-reader or just desiring to upgrade into a newer model, the Kindle Paperwhite e-reader is an ideal option for you. Other than the knowledge about the new features, this e-publication provides simplest ways of benefiting from the Kindle Paperwhite. Therefore, create an account with Amazon and be the lucky one to enjoy the categorical benefits of this device that is currently hitting the market with a bang. Do not remain behind in this digital world.

CHAPTER ONE: Special Features Of The Kindle Paperwhite E-Reader

Understanding the properties that best describe this latest Paperwhite is relevant to prove that you just got what you wanted and that you have not wasted any of your hard-earned cents.

Ever since the Kindle e-reader was invented in the year 2007, Amazon has invested handsomely in updating its features. These features make the device ideal for those who do not have a jurisdiction and regulated schedule when it comes to reading. However, depending on the different customer preferences, this Kindle Paperwhite comes in different colors. For example, the Kindle Paperwhite e-reader Black comes with a stylish black color to attract many customers who are in love with the dark shadings.

With these features inclined in this device, the Kindle Paperwhite reads the same way as paper, only that it has the benefit of not hurting your eyes when the sun is shining. During the nights, one can continue reading because of the special **backlight** feature of the Kindle Paperwhite.

The outstanding display technology of this device rates it better than the basic Kindle.

The Kindle Paperwhite is slim and attractive to its users

6-inch Carta E Ink HD touchscreen display

Just like the highly ranked e-readers like the Kindle Voyage and the Kobo Glo HD, the 6-inch Kindle Paperwhite e-reader has an E- Ink screen with 300 pixels per inch resolution. This is twice the basic Kindle. Because of this, the screen delivers sharp texts with strong contrast as well. This makes the texts appear a bit crisper and with laser quality.

Because of the inbuilt lighting system, this device is considered to be in a league of its own. This balances the whiteness of the paper when reading. This is adjustable to match the time of the day you are using the e-reader.

The screen, as an advantage, comes in three layers in order to enhance an amazing and comfortable experience. The screen is sensitive ad responsive enough to improve your experience.

Unlike the Voyage Kindle, the user navigates the book via this touchscreen in Paperwhite.

Four low-powered LED lights

To enable you to read during the nights or in dark places, this technological device has a four LED lights that project over the covers. This prevents one from straining when reading the book under the undesirable dark conditions.

The low-power property of the lighting system boosts the battery life since it consumes less voltage compared to several other e-readers with lighting systems. Because of this, the Kindle Paperwhite lasts for weeks before the need to recharge it.

Anti-glare property

Reading under a glaring sun is discomforting to the readers and might as well affect the optical health. To avert these effects, Amazon has updated this Paperwhite e-reader with an astonishing property that protects the reader against the harmful sun rays when one is reading out into the sun.

Prolonged battery life

Every person would desire to purchase an e-reader that lasts before the need to recharge it. The Kindle Paperwhite is, therefore, ideal when you need to acquire a Kindle. The advantageous properties like the low-powered LED lights consume less energy thereby heightening the battery life.

Research by Amazon indicates that when fully charged, Kindle Paperwhite e-reader can last for up to two weeks. However, when you regulate your reading to about an hour daily with the wireless connection off and the lighting set at about 10, the charge can last for up to six weeks in the event of a single charge.

4GB built-in memory with 512MB RAM

The Kindle Paperwhite is referred to as a library of books. This is because it can hold millions of book titles despite the fact that it is small. With this device, you can download many books and store them in the 4GB memory available.

Even with the lack of time, you can consider the upgraded 512MB RAM that boosts the downloading speed to be convenient for you.

Both the 3G+Wi-Fi or Wi-Fi options

The basic Kindles come with only a Wi-Fi connectivity. However, this upgraded Kindle comes with either the 3G+Wi-Fi or Wi-Fi options for the users to choose from. According to the majority of users, the 3G is the most convenient for downloading the many books from Amazon.

Because of this, Amazon provides the 3G services in more than 100 countries at no extra cost. Amazon opted to this after finding out that Wi-Fi and hotspots are not always reliable. This property has made it easy for the users of these devices to browse books as well as downloading several other copies. This is a huge boost for the traveling readers globally because whenever you travel, the 3G network is with you wherever you are.

Made of matte, soft-touch plastic

Just like any other Kindle, this Paperwhite e-reader is light and portable. To be specific, this up-to-date device is made of matte plastic that gives a soft touch compared to others. This material is responsible for its lightweight (about 205g for the Wi-Fi version and 217g for that with both the 3G and Wi-Fi versions). Because of this, you can hold this device for long without feeling the weight on your hand.

As an advantage, the device also has a number of grips to enable the users to have a comfortable grasp. A chunky bezel that surrounds this display gives the fingers of the handler somewhere to rest when using it.

CHAPTER TWO: Setting up Your Amazon Kindle Paperwhite E-Reader

With digital book revolution, Amazon provides us with a variety of e-readers that make it an easy and interesting experience to read the various browsed or downloaded books. Operating these devices is pretty easy in case one has knowledge on how to set the system ready for use.

Before beginning to make use of the e-reader, there are specific activities that must be taken into consideration to ensure the setup operates efficiently. For example, it is mandatory to create an account with Amazon or synchronize it with an existing one before beginning to take advantage of the device.

1. Charging your Kindle

Once you unbox the device, you will need to charge it before turning it on. Fortunately, every Kindle including the Amazon Kindle Paperwhite comes with its own USB charger. With this, you can connect it to either a switched on PC or a laptop.

Though the Kindle keyboard also comes with a mains charger, it is important noting that the Kindle Paperwhite or any other Kindle ought to be connected to the USB socket on the PC since it is likely not to charge when inserted through the hub or keyboard.

Most Kindle holders purchase a mains power charger that comes with a USB connection. Next to the USB socket is a LED that indicates whether the e-reader is fully charged. That is, the LED glows yellow when the charging is in the process but when it is fully charged, the glowing changes to green. In addition to this, the LED lights spread evenly on the device for convenient reading of the book even in dark conditions. This makes the Kindle Paperwhite the best –ink screen available on the current market.

Unless the device is in a sleep mode or turned off, the LED lights never go off. However, this does not affect the battery life since it consumes extremely less energy to be able to alter the up to six weeks battery life following a full charge.

Unfortunately, the Kindle Paperwhite does not come with a power adapter for the wall. This means that for recharging, it is only possible to connect it to a computer.

2. Switching on your Kindle

Once the LED glows green, it is now time to begin enjoying the value of your cash. Just next to the USB port is a power switch that will initiate the journey to your new and amazing experience. The device is turned on by just sliding and releasing the switch. This power-on button is the only button on this device.

In case you are impatient to allow your device to charge fully, it is possible to use it while still attached to the PC via the USB port. To activate this in Windows Visa or Windows 7, select the Computer from the Start Menu, right-click upon the icon of the Kindle and then press **Eject**. However, in case you are using a Windows XP, right-click on the **safely remove hardware** on the right-hand side of the taskbar to continue enjoying your value.

In case you desire to turn it off, it is required that you slide the switch and hold it for about four seconds until you see the screen turning black. Sliding the switch and letting it go will just put the device to sleep rather than switching it off. Subsequent sliding of the switch and letting it go would again wake it up. Therefore, hold the switch for the speculated time until it goes off suddenly.

For a new Kindle, a display will appear on the screen to give you the options of getting started. Follow, therefore, the onscreen instructions to help you connect to the Wi-Fi and then register your device.

The switch I just next to the USB port.

3. Network connection

With the devices coming with Wi-Fi or with both the Wi-Fi and 3G options, the initial step to take before benefiting from this upgraded reading library is to connect your Kindle to any available network.

To connect to any network, go to **menu**> **settings**> **Wi-Fi Network**, scan for any available network then enter the password to begin enjoying your e-reader. This also applies to a public hotspot. Your gadget recognizes the available Wi-Fi network using a WPS compatible router. To enable this procedure of connecting via the WPS, first select the **wireless network** of your choice, and then press the **WPS** button on your router before again selecting the **WPS** once again in order to display the strength of your network signal via the indicator.

For those devices that have both the Wi-Fi and 3G options, you can skip the Wi-Fi setup for now and make use of its in-built cellular 3G connection. However, some users prefer to add their own personal network (either Wi-Fi or hotspot) to improve the connectivity. This is because the added network is usually faster than the cellular connection. Once your connection is active, it is now time to begin the next step in ensuring you enjoy the benefits of this special gadget. Unfortunately, it is important to note that this device does not support the ad hoc Wi-Fi network. That is peer-to-peer Wi-Fi network.

Just like our phones, a 3G gadget would automatically connect to the 3G signal depending on its strength. In the case of a weaker strength, the Kindle would connect to the relatively slower EDGE or the GPRS network. In the presence of any Wi-Fi available, the 3G automatically turns off, but when the Wi-Fi is turned off, the Kindle will automatically switch back to 3G.

With the need to turn off the wireless connection, turn on the **Airplane Mode** to put into a hold all downloads in a process that require the wireless connection. The downloading processes will continue the next time you turn off the Airplane Mode.

In case you have difficulties when connecting to your network, please contact your network administrator or even those individuals responsible for maintaining your preferred network.

4. Registering your Kindle Paperwhite e-reader

The outstanding Kindle Paperwhite e-reader is an Amazon product that improves our reading experience. With this in mind, it is important to register your device with the Amazon to ensure maximum utilization of this technology.

However, for those who have purchased this e-reader online using Amazon, the gadget comes when it is registered already. Confirming the registration is, therefore, mandatory to put your ownership and your utilization of this Kindle to enhance your intended goal of a greater and fantastic reading experience. That is, in case you click the **Home** icon and observe that the top left corner of your device says "My Kindle" or in case it shows the name of the previous owner, then you need to begin the registration process with immediate effects.

Registering this device takes a series of steps that ought to be considered professionally. This depends on whether the Kindle had previously been registered or not. To determine this, go to the **Setting page** then select the **Registration and Household** option. In case the device was initially registered, deregister it then begin the reregistration process once again.

During this registration processes, enable the sign in approval then enter your secret passcode before keying in an additional security code sent to your phone once you complete the registration process.

In case you do not have an Amazon account, create yours from your PC. Simply select **Create an account** from your Kindle. With this account set up, sign up using your Amazon.co.uk username and password then click the **OK** to enjoy your device.

5. Safeguarding your books

Once your Kindle is all set, it is now time to stop others from accessing your content. Setting up a password is the easiest way of ensuring this. This makes it difficult to access the contents of the device once it goes to sleep unless you key in the correct passcode.

To set up the security code, press the **Home** followed by the **Menu** icon. Select the **Settings** and scroll down to the **Device Password** option. Choose the **Turn on** option and type the password of your own choice. Lest you forget, it is also important to assign a password hint to help you recall your passcode.

Be assured that your device is protected from intruders by pressing the **Submit** option. This confirms your password and switches it on.

In case your kids also use the Kindle, consider setting up a parental control to avoid them from accidentally purchasing the books.

6. Setting up a payment method

The Kindle Paperwhite is useful in helping you browse and read a number of eBooks. Starting a payment option is, therefore, important to make it easy for you to purchase the various books of your choice.

To do this, visit the **Manage Your Kindle page** using your Kindle web browser. When on the Home Screen, open the **Home Menu** and then select the **Experimental.**

Normally, all the Amazon Kindles use the Amazon's 1 –click Payment method to help its users purchase the various books of their choice. This method uses either the debit or credit card with your default shipping address in your Amazon account.

To customize your payment option, select your 1-Click payment method then press **Edit.** Either select or add a new debit or credit card you desire to use for the 1-Click payment. Click the **Continue** icon to be assured that your changes are saved.

7. Shop eBooks for your Kindle

Once all is set, it is now the right time to begin purchasing the books your desire to read using your Kindle. To begin, click the **Menu** icon and then choose the **Shop in Kindle** to help you browse the Amazon's eBook selection.

In order to download a book, simply press the **Buy** option to feed your e-reader. Provided your Kindle is connected to a network (either Wi-Fi or 3G), the book will automatically download and store on your device.

In case you have a 3G Kindle, simply email the books directly to your device. To get your Kindle email, go to the **Menu**, then **Settings,** then the **Device Options** at the bottom of your screen you will see the email address to use.

8. Playing Around

It becomes easy to use the Kindle Paperwhite when you are used to using it. Other than the Amazon's Kindle model, a touchscreen device enables you to tap to reveal more pages.

To manage this, touch the top of the screen to disclose a toolbar, where the mostly used features such as the light control, the reading options, shopping, font sizes, go-to as well as the X-ray are included.

This is important for the new users of Kindle Paperwhite. This familiarizes them with the features for maximum utility of the product.

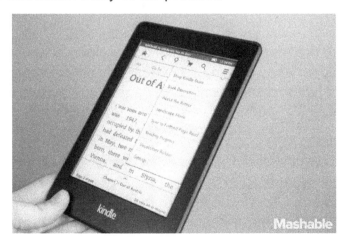

CHAPTER THREE: Reading the Various Books on Your Kindle Paperwhite

The Amazon Kindles play a good job in displaying the various eBooks on its monochrome screen. With an Amazon account, it has become easy for the lovers of these devices to browse various publications and download them into their Kindle.

Paperwhite is not limited to reading newspapers, books and magazines downloaded or bought from Amazon, but also allows you to read your own personal documents.

However, these documents come in various formats: HTML files, docx format, PDF files, rich text files (RTF) and image formats like the jpg, gif, bmp and png. This e-reader supports natively the PDF and the TXT files. The other document types that are not supported need to be converted into formats that can be read on your device.

There are many ways of getting your documents into Kindle for easy reading. This depends on the various listed types of file you need to transfer to the Kindle or rather the proximity of your Kindle to the computer.

Other than the browsed files, it is possible to read your own desired documents, books or articles on the Kindle regardless of their format. This is so because of the **send-to-kindle** feature that moves your contents into these devices or even the apps.

Because of the inability of the Kindle BlackBerry, the Windows Phone app, and the Windows 8 app among others to use the send-to-Kindle property, there are reliable sending options for your books, articles or the documents.

✓ **Sending By Email**

The initial step before using this easy sending option is a little setup. To do this, go to **Manage Your Content & Devices** on Amazon. On the far right, click on the **Settings** then scroll down until to reach your **Send-to-Kindle email settings**. From this point, you will notice a list of options (each with its own email address) to send your personal contents.

However, it is only possible to send your contents to the found devices' email addresses only when using an approved email. With this in mind, to protect your device, further scroll down until you find the **Approved Personal Documents E-mail List** section. From this point, only add the emails you wish to send your personal content from.

You are able to send multiple files in a single message when using this emailing method to send your documents.

Once the content is converted into Kindle format (AZW3) ad sent to your device, it is possible to manipulate the font size, margins, and line spacing to meet your taste.

✓ **Dragging and Dropping Via the USB**

Once you connect the Paperwhite Kindle to the computer using the Paperwhite's micro-USB to USB cable, your Kindle would appear as a storage device on the computer.

To send your personal content, simply drag the document from the computer and then drop it to the Kindle using the computer's Windows Explorer.

This method is cost-effective since, unlike using the email, no charge is required for transferring the content.

Unfortunately, this sending option is not reliable since it works only with the native file formats such as the PDF and TXT.

✓ Sending to the Kindle App

With a number of users disliking the email method, they prefer utilizing the **Send-to-Kindle** desktop application. With this method, your local documents are easily transferred to the Kindle without experiencing the stress of creating an email.

The first thing involved is to download the app on your PC and then install it. Once this is done, you get three different sending options to choose from: the **print dialog**, the **right-click menu** or the **drag-and-drop** option.

For example, in the Windows Explorer, right-click the file. This will bring the right-click context menu from which you select the Send-to-Kindle option.

This is the best sending options for those documents saved on your computer.

✓ Sending By Browser

For those users who wish to send the web pages, blog posts and articles to their Kindles, the browser extension provides the best alternative.

First download the extension (either the Chrome or Firefox), after which you select the Kindle to which you want to send the online material for future reading.

The next step entails identifying the article you desire to send. Using either the **Preview & Send** or **the Send-to-Kindle** options, transfer the content to your preferred device. From this point, you can now enjoy your book or article on your Kindle.

✓ **Sending By Android**

Though it is possible for the iOS users to receive the Send-to-Kindle content, one can only send them when using the Android media. This is so because the Android has an option for sharing the content, unlike the iOS.

It is mandatory to install the Kindle Android app after you have downloaded it on your PC before enjoying the benefits that come along with this app.

Once you tap the **Share** icon within any app within your computer, simply select the **Send-to-Kindle** option, and then choose the device you need to send the document to.

Reading the Epub Books on your Kindle

Epub format is an open and free eBook format that just like the web pages, can be edited using a web page editor. However, as earlier stated, the Amazon

Kindle Paperwhite is not able to support the Epub files.

Luckily enough, the documents in the Epub format downloaded from either AbeBooks, eBooks.com or the Google Books among the many other different online collection, can be converted to a uniform format (MOBI format) that can be supported on our Kindle. Once converted into a readable format by your e-reader, the books will appear on your Amazon Kindle book menu just like any other Kindle eBook. This is facilitated by various software available online such as the Calibre (considered the simplest option).

To initiate the conversion of the Epub documents, ensure your device is connected to a computer with this eBook management software program (the Calibre). This program works with the Mac, Linux as well as the Windows. Once installed into the PC, leave the Calibre checked to initiate the program right away. Any time you connect your e-reader to the computer with this software, your Kindle will be detected and automatically perform the desired conversion for easy reading.

On your computer, click the **Add Books** in order to add the Epub books to the Calibre eBook management system. To do this, browse to the folder in which the books are and select the document or books you desire.

When you are done adding your chosen books to the conversion system, it is now time to connect your device. Once detected, a new icon at the top of Calibre known as the **Send to Device** appears at the top of the eBook management system. Simply click this option to highlight the books or other documents you wish to send to your Kindle.

To finalize the job, you will be prompted to Auto-convert the files. When you see this notification, simply click the **Yes** and that's it. Your document is readable now. To confirm this, you will see at the bottom-right of the program, a status of the jobs in the process. Disconnect your device in case the number reads zero and begin enjoying your book content.

Reading the PDF Documents on Your Kindle Paperwhite E-Reader

For the lovers and long-term users of this software, you must be aware that this updated Kindle (Amazon Paperwhite Kindle) would not only support the eBooks, but also the PDFs. Unlike the Epub files, the PDFs do not require any software to convert them into their readable formats.

With the Kindle's own email, it is possible to send whatever PDF file right to your device as an attachment. Go to the Kindle's settings area to obtain the Kindle email through which you can send the files. All the Amazon Kindles have the ability to convert the PDF into readable raw text upon typing the word **convert** in the subject line of the mail.

This alternative, however, does not work perfectly according to some users who claim that they have a problem converting the PDF images and tables.

However, for those stubborn PDFs, a more reliable converter such as the Calibre prove to be useful.

Unfortunately, such software can only be installed on the PCs, and hence they are not useful when you are away from your computer.

To read the PDF content, first, connect your Kindle to the computer. Immediately the Kindle is connected, the drive will show up on the PC's **My Computer**. During this time, the screen changes to USB display to mean that you should now operate the device from the computer.

From the computer, open the Kindle drive and locate the **documents** folder. Once this is done, copy the PDF files and paste them in this folder. At this moment, the new PDF (looking great) will show up on your Kindle. Now you can disconnect the Kindle after ejecting it using the **Safely Remove Hardware** icon.

Depending on how the different PDFs are formatted, some of the final files look great while others are not. It is possible to customize the size of the display on your Kindle during the conversion process without altering the table of contents. Other than the panning procedures, this customization can best be done when you 'reverse pinch' on the device screen to zoom in on the content.

Basing on the quality of the original document, you may desire to adjust the PDF display to darken the print bit using the **font** menu.

CHAPTER FOUR: Managing Kindle Content

With the many confusing options included in the Amazon account, it is difficult to decide on what to do next with your Kindle. Knowing how to manage the device is an important step in ensuring you get the best of the e-reader. This chapter will provide you with all the facts and procedures necessary for the proper management of your content.

For example, you might either have accidentally deleted a book from your Kindle or rather wish to send few of your personal books to your Kindle. Whichever the reason might be, having knowledge on how to have command over your Kindle content will save a great deal to ensure you enjoy the maximum benefits.

For easy access to your Kindle books to Amazon customers, special authors need to understand the specific guideline on how to deliver quality Kindle content.

You might as well be wondering about the steps involved in managing your already existing Kindle library. This would no longer be a headache since all the necessary information is provided in this chapter.

Due to some unspecific reasons, one might be having access to a device not registered to his or her Amazon account. It is possible to change ownership by deregistering the existing account and replacing it with your own.

The **Manage Your Content Devices** icon provides all the required options for any type of management you might desire for your Kindles including the least expected setting a Kindle Family Library.

A. Replacing an Existing Amazon Account

Earlier in chapter two of this book, it was stated that there is a possibility of deregistering a Kindle registered to a wrong account and reregistering it afresh.

This chapter, however, gives specific guidelines for its users to follow in case they experience this circumstance. That is, it is important to provide the procedure on how to replace an existing account for the benefit of the Kindle users.

❖ Deregistering Your Kindle Paperwhite

Before signing to a new account, there is need to remove the existing one before any process transpires. This can be because either the device was registered to a wrong Amazon account or you no longer wish to use it for the purchasing of new content.

This process entails a series of procedures that ought to be followed keenly. In addition to this, the device must be connected to a wireless network before the deregistration journey begins.

To perform this process via your PC:

i. Visit the **Manage Your Content and Devices** icon.

ii.   Secondly, select **Your Devices** and then from here, select the **Your Devices and App** before clicking the **Deregister** from within the Action column.

iii. To confirm this whole process, it is required that you again select the **Deregister** that appears in the pop-up window.

Similarly, in case you want to perform the process from your Kindle, the following is an easy to follow the procedure:

i.   When **Home**, click the **Menu** icon to locate the **Settings** option.

ii.   Scroll and tap the **Registration** icon from where you will see the **Deregister Your Kindle** dialog box.

iii. Tap the **Deregister** to confirm the deregistration process.

Once your device is deregistered, it is now time to reregister it to your new account.

❖ **Reregistering Your Kindle Paperwhite**

Once you deregister your Kindle from the old account, you cannot access any material from Amazon. This means that you will not be able to have a glance at the content from your Kindle Library or even the content that you had previously downloaded.

It is, therefore, important you register your device afresh once you deregister it from the outdated account. It is on this account that one is able to buy or even deliver the Kindle content to his or her device.

This process as well requires connection to a wireless network.

i.   From the **Home** icon, select the **Menu**.
ii.   From the options that emerge from the Menu, select the **Settings** and then tap the **Registration** option.
iii.   The final procedure is selecting an Amazon account you would wish to use with your Kindle Paperwhite:

- In case you have an existing account, tap the **If you already have an Amazon account** option to enter your credentials (email and password) linked with the Amazon account.

  Tap the **Register** and see your name appearing as the Registered User upon the completion of the registration process.

- Similarly, for the newbies (those without an Amazon account), it is advised that you tap the **If you do not have an Amazon account** then follow the easy to follow the procedure that follows on the screen to set your own account for registration.

With your Kindle now registered to your own account, it is now possible to access all the Kindle content from Amazon as well as use the Kindle to read your own personal eBooks, newspapers, and magazines among other publications.

B. Managing Documents in the Kindle Library

Just as for any other management procedure of your Kindle, the first step involved here is signing into your Amazon account and then clicking the **Manage Your Kindle Content and Devices** at the top of your Kindle screen. From this option, the page is divided into three parts: **Your Content**, **Your Devices,** and **the Settings**.

Of the three, select **Your Content**. Here you can either add or delete the Kindle content:

- To deliver the Kindle documents, select the titles you want to deliver (from the list of books that appear) by checking the box next to that particular heading and click **Deliver**. From the list, select the device you want to send the document and again click **Deliver** to complete the process.
- However, in case you desire to remove certain content from the Kindle, from the **Manage Your Content and Devices page**, choose the titles you need to delete then click the **Delete** and then confirm by clicking the **Yes, Delete**.

In case you do not desire the content to automatically store in the Manage Your Content and Devices, then instantly disable the automatic document archiving. This is done by following a series of steps that are as well easy to follow:

- Visit the **Manage Your Content and Devices**
- Of the three options, select **Settings** tab and down scroll to **Personal Document Settings**.
- Under the **Personal Document Archiving**, choose the Edit Archive Settings.

- Next, you will see the box next to **Enable personal document archiving to my Kindle library** checked. Uncheck the box then click **Update** to confirm the disabling process.

In case you need to archive the documents, simply check the box adjacent to **Enable personal document archiving to my Kindle library** then click the **Update** option.

C. Setting Up Kindle Family Library

This guide provides procedure on how to enhance the privacy of your eBooks within your Kindle. However, Amazon, as well allows family members to share the Kindle app, books and more. This is made possible by the help of the **Family Library** feature (supported only by the latest Kindle Paperwhite e-reader). Setting up this software is so confusing to operate and hence maximum concentration is demanded during this period.

To begin, confirm that your device is compatible with the Kindle Family Library. This is done by checking the Amazon's **Family compatibility page**. In addition to this, you will also be able to realize the minimum number of software your device require for it to access the Family Library content. To make the feature to function, you at least require one Kindle that can support it if not all.

The next phase is making sure your Kindles possesses the latest software updates. This is done by tapping the menu>Settings>menu>Device Info. Locate the individual devices on Amazon's **Kindle**

software updates page to confirm whether the version number matches.

In order to set up a Family Library on a Kindle that supports the managing Family Library settings, from the **Menu**, tap the **Settings** then the **Registration and Household**. From here, tap the **Household and Family Library**. From this screen, create a 'Household' then add both the Amazon email address and passwords of every person you want to share your library with. The books to be shared have to be selected by the creator of the Family Library.

After the whole process, go to the Books section. From here, you should observe new book entries shared by your family members. Other than this, you must receive a confirmation email to verify the newly created "Household."

This makes Amazon Kindle Paperwhite e-reader a special device since it can support the **Family Library** feature.

D. Managing Your Kindle Content from the Amazon Website

It is possible to have command over your Kindle via the Amazon website. To do this, follow the following easy-to-follow guidelines:

From the drop-down menu next to **Your Account**, select the **Manage Your Content and Devices**.

Select the **Your Content** to list your library of books. Select the book you would wish to remove then click the **Action**. Clicking this **Action** precedes a pop-out menu that provides options beyond the **delete** and

delivers. That is, you can for example, add narration, further page reading, transfer content via the USB as well as downloading the title you desire.

Importantly, to manage the various Amazon Kindles and Kindle mobile apps, select **Your Devices** instead of the **Your Content**.

Again, on the aforementioned Settings page, you can edit the payment method, changing your country settings as well as managing any subscription and the synchronization or whisper sync settings.

The **Language Optimized Storefront** option enables you to view your Kindle in your desired language (for example native language).

For those who prefer sending their Kindles via the email, the user needs to add the Kindle address you wish to send the material to in the **Approved Personal Document Email List**. This is mandatory to help the address be received on your device.

It is as well possible to form a Family Library on the Amazon website. Create a 'Household' then invite the adult. For the children and other adults, select the options from **Manage Your Content and Devices page** from this Amazon site then follow the easy-to-follow procedure. That is, adults will need to sign into their Amazon accounts, but just create profiles for children and let them enjoy the shared content.

E. Using the Kindle Paperwhite Built-In Browser

With the characteristic built-in browser of the Kindle Paperwhite e-reader, the users are able to access the internet anytime regardless of where they are.

Though the built-in web browser of the device is simpler to that of the computer, it comes with astonishing features that make it unique from the one from that of the computer:

The web browser has the ability to connect to the internet conveniently at any time you are in a Wi-Fi hotspot. Other than this, the 3G wireless, though limited to Amazon or Wikipedia, is free to access. This makes it a cost-effective browser for its users. The 3G wireless is functional for those who are in areas covered by the AT&T cellular data network (network used by the Kindle Paperwhite).

The Kindle Paperwhite web browser enhances the access to the eBook and blogs website links you desire to know more about.

The Kindle Paperwhite web browser displays, in either the address bar, the URL, or web address of the web page previously accessed using the bookmark feature.

How to Get Online

To be connected to the internet using the device browser, follow the following steps:

- Tap the Menu icon from the Home screen.
- The next step is tapping the Experimental Browser option.

- Once this is done, a list of website bookmarks appears on the screen, some including Google, Wikipedia, New York Times and with Amazon at the top of the list. Therefore, to open a bookmarked page in the browser, tap one of the listed bookmarks.

Managing the Bookmarks

Other than saving the web pages, bookmarking also help to avoid re-entering extremely long URLs from the onscreen keyboard of the Kindle Paperwhite. This involves adding a bookmark, accessing the saved bookmark, bookmark editing and deleting a bookmark.

a) Adding a bookmark

To enhance this, first, tap the **Menu** then select the **Bookmark This Page**.

b) Accessing your saved bookmarks

It is possible to save web pages for future reference. Bookmarking makes this operation an easy one.

- ✓ Tap the Menu icon
- ✓ Click on the **Bookmarks** to visit the preloaded sample bookmarks by Amazon.

c) Deleting a bookmark

The initial steps are aimed at opening the saved bookmarks on your Kindle then.

- ✓ Check the boxes that appear next to the displayed bookmark (it is possible to check more than one bookmark).

✓ To delete the selected bookmark, tap **Remove** to complete the operation.

d) Editing a bookmark

At the bottom of bookmarks screen after opening the saved pages, tap **Edit** then the **Bookmark** to edit the name of the bookmark.

Browser Special Settings

It is not always necessary to fear about the default settings of your Kindle Paperwhite's web browser. However, there may arise the need to reset the Kindle in order to resolve some of the problems identified, including improving the browsing speed from one page to another.

For these special settings, tap the **Menu** then choose the **Browser Setting**. Tapping this option further provide the following options:

- **Clear Cookies**

Cookies are small strings of information saved by the web pages. For the Kindle Paperwhite e-reader, the information is stored on the hard drive. These cookies can, for example, be used to save the login details.

To clear this information, consider the Clear Cookies option. This might be done for those browsers that respond very slowly or does not respond at all.

- **Clear History**

One special feature of the Kindle Paperwhite is to save the URLs, and all the web pages content visited previously.

These saved histories make the web browser extremely slow and hence the need to delete them. This is made possible following the Clear History option.

- ○ **Disabling images**

For unspecified reasons, your web browser will be slow in internet connection. This will, as a result, make the web page graphics and pictures to load slowly.

Tapping the Disable Images option enables you to delete the images, leaving only the text content of the webpage for viewing.

- ○ **Disabling JavaScript**

For enhanced functionality like the submenus, a number of websites use the JavaScript. Disabling this JavaScript is a special setting that should be considered in case the web browser responds slowly.

F. Managing the Article Mode

Swiping the article display on Kindle Paperwhite to scroll up and down enhances the viewing of the articles. This works well with a number of new sites.

In order to turn off this Article Mode, tap the **Menu** then the **Web Mode**.

CHAPTER FIVE: Get More from Your Kindle Paperwhite

The Amazon Kindle Paperwhite enables the user to walk with a library in his or her pocket. However smaller and lighter the device might look, this e-reader comes with special features that help the user personalize the device (some of which are explained in the earlier chapters).

Understanding the properties and some quick tricks make it possible to get the best out of your Kindle. This chapter entails those unknown properties and tips on how to use your e-readers that most users are ignorant of. For example, the built-in tools, third party software, the Kindle supercharge as well as the other experimental features.

To sum this all, there are also some tips and tricks that when taken into keen consideration, will enhance your personal experience and let you benefit more from your Kindle Paperwhite.:

Enhance the battery life

It is stated that the average duration for an off charge Kindle is about six weeks. This duration can be enhanced further by personalizing your device. That is, setting the device to cut its energy consumption.

To do this, for example, it is required that you switch your device into an airplane mode in case you are not using it to download. Turning off the wireless connection entails tapping the **Settings** and eventually turning on the **Airplane Mode** from here.

Customizing the display fonts

Some content comes with hard-to-read font display. With Kindle Paperwhite, however, this should not be a problem any longer.

By the help of your fingers, make a "spread" gesture to increase the font size of your Kindle display. On the same note, "pinch" the screen using your fingers to make the display font size small to see more words as a result.

Dictionary customization

The content of the eBook might come in a foreign language and hence make it a challenge for some of its users. To manage this issue, go to **Settings**, then **Device Options**, then **Language and Dictionaries**. This will translate the content into a language clearly understood by the user.

Taking screenshots

Saving an image or a page for future reference can sometimes be a headache. The Kindle Paperwhite e-reader, however, comes with its ability to take screenshots feature to help in this area.

To take a screenshot and share them electronically, simply press down the **Alt, Shift,** and **g.** Alternatively, either you can hold the top right/bottom left combination or the top left/bottom right combination to take the screenshot.

Once this is done, connect your Kindle to the computer using the USB cable and copy it from the **document** folder.

Customize your Kindle screensaver

The default screensaver of the Kindle Paperwhite might not be attractive to some of its users and hence the desire to change it with an image of their own choice.

To jailbreak your screensaver, install the jailbreak and the screensaver **hack**. The hack works on every Kindle including the Paperwhite e-reader except for the first generation devices. With this installation, you can customize as many images as your screensaver as possible.

Personalizing your device

Personalization of your device makes it unique. This can be done by customizing the name of your device with a name of your choice (preferably a name that reflects your personality).

N/B: changing the design and size of the font display is also a way personalizing your device.

CHAPTER SIX: The Essential Kindle Paperwhite E-Reader's Timesaving Tricks and ALT Shortcuts

In the earlier chapters, special guidelines are provided to make it easy for the newbies to operate this technological e-reader. This, however, might seem confusing to the operator or sometimes take much of their time.

With this in mind, this chapter has analyzed the Kindle Paperwhite to discover the shortcuts to various setting operations of this device. The Alt Shortcuts make operating this device an easy endeavor.

To be specific, this chapter provides the reading shortcuts, the note-taking shortcuts, audio shortcuts, shopping as well as searching for books from the Home Page among many others.

1. The Alt Shortcuts for an effective reading experience

Different publications might come in varying display fonts and line spacing. This makes it difficult for some users to grasp the best of the content quality. However, with the Kindle Paperwhite e-reader, it is possible to change the line spacing if you do not feel comfortable reading the existing display. To further this advantage, a simple use of the **Shift** and **Alt** icons will make you customize the screen display for your own personal interest. That is, clicking the **Shift-Alt 1-9** would help in changing the line spacing depending on your desire.

In addition to this, it is sometimes important to save some of the pages for future references. To do this, bookmarking of the pages you need to save is vital. To do this, however, clicking the **Alt-B** will make it an easy operation for you to have a future reference. This is a better alternative than the analog clicking the **Menu** and the **Bookmark This Page** as illustrated in the earlier chapter of this handy guidebook. Once saved, it is possible to revisit the pages anytime you desire as well as deleting it when you feel like you no longer need it.

At times, the screen display may appear to be faded or with some undesirable shadows that make it unpleasant to grasp the content of the eBook. To manage this, it is advisable to refresh the page for a clearer display by just clicking the **Alt-G**.

2. The essential note-taking shortcuts

Other than just reading, the Kindle Paperwhite allows the users to take important notes for future reference. This is one of the many reasons as to why you should attempt to acquire this device as soon as possible.

During the note-taking exercise, the SYM displays all the symbols for effective punctuation and understanding of the notes taken in the process. By the help of the **Alt** icon, it is important to include the symbols without having to locate them from the SYM display. Below are some of the most used symbols and the shortcuts to apply them:

- ✓ Clicking the **Alt 6** translates to the question mark (?)
- ✓ Clicking the **Alt 7** translates to a comma (,)

✓ Clicking the **Alt 8** translates to a colon (:)
✓ Clicking the **Alt 9** translates to a quotation mark (")
✓ Clicking the **Alt 0** translates to the apostrophe (')

Having knowledge about the above shortcuts among the many other makes note taking much easier with the Paperwhite Kindle.

3. Searching the books from the Home Page

The Kindle is referred to as a library of books due to its ability to store millions of titles. Keeping track of your stored eBooks can be so hectic. It is, therefore, important to organize your library in a suitable format as directed by the Amazon Kindle Paperwhite guidebooks. That is an organization by the built-in methods which can be sorting either by titles or by the type of item.

Accessing the different books or even the specific pages of an eBook, there are shortcuts that makes this much easier than scrolling down to it:

❖ **The personalized search using the search function**

With the many books within the e-reader, it is possible to search for the book you desire to read. This is made easy by the **search function** of the Paperwhite e-reader from the Homepage. Simply click the first letter of a number of the book you need to have a look at.

❖ **Skipping the books or pages alphabetically**

From the Homepage, it is a list of books stored in your Kindle are listed for easy access to them. Accessing a specific book becomes easy by simply clicking the first letter, from the SYM, of the book Author or title depending on the format in which the library was organized.

In addition to this, the 5-way controller makes it even easier for the locating the books or pages of your choice. This is done by scrolling to either to the **sort by Title or Author name** or the **Page number** respectively. This is found on the right of the screen display.

The 5-way controller can, however, be used as well to scroll to the left in order to sort the content by the **type of item** stored.

4. Shortcuts to shop for an eBook

When you suddenly feel like downloading a new book, simply click the **Alt Home** to open the Kindle Book Store and then select the book you desire to purchase from Amazon.

In case the network connection is not effective to help you purchase the book, simply click the **Alt-R** to reload the web page from which you are acquiring the book.

5. Shortcuts to manage the Kindle audio

Other than reading, you can use your eBook to listen to music when you feel like relaxing your mind. The various manufacturers' manuals provide the guidelines on how to manage the mobile music system.

However, the following shortcuts make it possible to control the audio:

- Clicking the **Alt Space** either starts or stops the music automatically.
- The **Alt-F** can be used to change to the next audio track.
- Clicking the **Shift-SYM** activates the **Text-to-Speech mode** (TTS).
- Tapping the **space bar** icon pauses or resumes the TTS

Other than the above approved shortcuts, there are other shortcuts and tricks that can make your use of the Kindle Paperwhite e-reader an interesting, easy and time-saving experience. These include the following:

- Clicking the **Alt-Z** when loading a picture folder will help in providing more information about the pictures.
- Considering the **Shift-Alt M** to switch to playing the Minesweeper in your Kindle.
- Clicking the Shift-Alt G is the easiest way of taking a screenshot of a page you need to save for future reference.
- Using the **5-way controller** to either right of the left can be helpful when you need to delete a book from the Homepage. This depends on the style of the e-reader book organization. Either by the names of the books' authors and title or the type of item respectively.

To, therefore, enjoy the value of your hard-earned cash, it is, therefore, to learn all the shortcuts to enhance your relationship with your Kindle.

CONCLUSION

It was a great decision purchasing this Amazon Kindle Paperwhite e-reader guidebook before starting to enjoy its benefits.

With all the explanations about the different features of this Amazon device, including the procedure to set it up, I believe you will reap the maximum output of the product.

Purchase this Kindle and be up-to-date with the technology.

Finally, if you enjoyed this book, please take the time to share your thoughts and post a review on Amazon. It would be greatly appreciated! Thank you and good luck!

CPSIA information can be obtained
at www.ICGtesting.com
Printed in the USA
BVHW052304210123
656830BV00013B/880